LMS Steam in the 1930s
The George Barlow Collection

Brian J. Dickson

© Images and Design: The Transport Treasury 2022. Text: Brian J. Dickson

ISBN 978-1-913893-23-1

First published in 2022 by Transport Treasury Publishing Ltd. 16 Highworth Close, High Wycombe, HP13 7PJ
Totem Publishing, an imprint of Transport Treasury Publishing.

www.ttpublishing.co.uk

Printed in Tarxien, Malta by Gutenberg Press Ltd.

'LMS Steam in the 1930s' is one of a series of books on specialist transport subjects published in strictly limited numbers and produced under the Totem Publishing imprint using material only available at The Transport Treasury.

Front Cover: Sunday 20 August 1939. At Crewe shed LMS Class 6P 'Royal Scot' 4-6-0 No 6100 *Royal Scot* is seen standing over an inspection pit. She had originally been constructed at Derby Works as No 6152 *Kings Dragoon Guardsman* during 1930 but swapped identities with the original No 6100 in 1933 prior to her departure to America to visit the Chicago Century of Progress Exhibition. Returning to the U.K. later that year, she retained the identity and would be rebuilt with a taper boiler during 1950 and be withdrawn from service in 1962. She managed to escape the cutters torch and is now owned by a trust and is to be seen working main line specials. (GB791)

Frontispiece: Wednesday 31 May 1933. The ex-LNWR 'Claughton' (LMS Class 5XP) 4-6-0's were a class of four-cylindered express passenger locomotives designed by Charles Bowen Cooke with No 6025, seen here at Nottingham Midland station being constructed at Crewe Works during 1921. This unnamed member of the class would have a short working life of only fourteen years being withdrawn in 1935. (GB703)

Rear Cover: Sunday 20 August 1939. Seen at Crewe Works and scheduled for withdrawal during the same month, former LNWR 'Square Tank' 0-6-0 No 27334 is bearing the name *Liverpool*. Originally constructed as a '17" Class' 0-6-0 tender locomotive commonly referred to as 'Coal Engines' she would be rebuilt during the George Whale period as an 0-6-0 tank. (GB789)

Photographer - George Barlow

Born in Nottingham in 1916, George developed a life-long interest in railways of all gauges and steam locomotives in particular. On leaving school, he tried to join the LNER as an engine cleaner at Colwick but they were recruiting fewer staff at that time and George was unlucky. Instead he joined the Nottingham Journal where he became a proofreader until being called up in 1940 when he applied to join the Railway Operating Department of the Royal Engineers and, to his surprise, was accepted. After his military training he served on the Melbourne Military Railway (a ten mile branch line between Chellaston Junction and Ashby-de-la-Zouch) where he learnt his footplate skills. Having passed out as a driver in 1941, he undertook diesel locomotive training and returned to the Melbourne Military Railway as a diesel instructor. Until demobilisation he worked on some ten military railways around the country, gaining experience on many types of steam and diesel locomotives and cranes.

George was unable to settle back in his old job at the Nottingham Journal as a proofreader and sought an opening as a locomotive driver but by now was too old to join the 'Big Four' so applied to an advert in the Model Railway magazine for a '…driver for a famous miniature railway…' but failing to get a reply he wrote to the General Manager of the Romney, Hythe and Dymchurch Railway asking if they had placed the advert, they hadn't but they did need a driver for the 1947 season and would he like to come for an interview? George duly got the job and he and his family moved into their new house at the Pilot Halt near Dungeness at the beginning of 1947, and the following year moved into a railway house in New Romney. He was made Foreman Driver at the end of the first season at New Romney and during the following years became the face of 'the friendly line'. In 1968 George was promoted to Operating Manager, the post he held until retirement in 1982 when he was awarded the British Empire Medal for his services to the RH&DR.

George bought his first camera in 1933 and was an enthusiastic photographer for seventy years. His collection includes many photographs taken around Nottingham together with others taken when out on his frequent cycling trips to other parts of the country.

George died in June 2006 and the above biographical notes were supplied by Paul Ross who also placed the George Barlow Collection of photographs with The Transport Treasury.

Paul Ross

Introduction

The 1930s were a period of rapid change for the LMS, the first of the Fowler designed 'Royal Scots' had arrived during 1927 and were quickly followed by the remainder of the class in 1930. In the same year the first of the 'Patriots', which were conceived as three-cylinder rebuilds of the four-cylinder 'Claughtons', entered service but these turned out to be new constructions with the bulk of the class being delivered into service between 1932 and 1934.

William Stanier joined the LMS in January 1932 and the first design created under his management was approved in April of that year for the 'Princess Royal' four-cylinder express passenger class intended for the traffic between London and Glasgow. The first of the class, No 6200 The Princess Royal, entered service during July 1933. Meanwhile the design for his three-cylinder 5XP class that became known as 'Jubilees' had been approved in May of that year with the first member, No 5552 Silver Jubilee, being delivered in May 1934. Hot on the heels of the 'Jubilee' class were delivered in August 1934 the first examples of his two-cylinder Class 5P5F, the 'Black Staniers' that became commonly known as the 'Black 5s'. With the LMS proposal to introduce non-stop services to Glasgow from London, the design of a new four-cylinder class, the 'Princess Coronation', was approved in July 1936 with the first member, No 6220 Coronation, entering service during June 1937 and the 'Coronation Scot' streamlined service being introduced between London and Glasgow in July of that year.

All these new classes started to replace the older LNWR express classes such as the 'Precursor', 'George the Fifth', 'Prince of Wales' and 'Claughton' locomotives, the greater bulk of which would have been withdrawn by the mid-1930s. Our photographer has captured images of many members of these classes before their demise and examples are included in the book.

Ex-Midland Railway locomotives still found much use with the LMS, who had in fact still been constructing examples of the two-cylinder 2P 4-4-0s and three-cylinder 'Compound' 4-4-0s throughout the late 1920s and early 1930s. Also entering service during the same period were the Fowler designed parallel boilered 2-6-2 and 2-6-4 tanks together with over five hundred of the ubiquitous 4F 0-6-0s based on the earlier Midland Railway design which were produced between 1923 and 1928 by three independent manufacturers and four LMS Workshops.

The compiler would wish to thank the Midland Railway Society for its assistance with details concerning a number of that railway's locomotives.

Brian J. Dickson

Saturday 10 June 1933. Departing from Rugby at the head of an express is George Whale designed 'Precursor' 4-4-0 No 5246 *Adjutant*. Constructed at Crewe Works during 1906 she would have the relatively short working life of only thirty years being withdrawn in 1936. (GB29)

Saturday 31 March 1934. The Francis Webb design of 2-4-2 tanks with 5' 6" driving wheels were introduced to the LNWR during 1890 with construction continuing until 1897 when a total of one hundred and sixty examples had entered service, all from Crewe Works. Designated Class 1P by the LMS, No 6658, seen here at Nuneaton, was one of the longest lived having been constructed in 1893 and withdrawn from service during 1950 numbered 46658 with British Railways. (GB56)

Tuesday 24 April 1934. Originally designed as a class of locomotive to handle commuter trains, the Richard Deeley Class 2000 0-6-4 tanks for the Midland Railway turned out to be poor performers with a tendency to be rough riders. A total of forty examples were constructed, all at Derby Works, during 1907 with No 2002, seen here at Nottingham Midland station, being withdrawn during 1937. (GB78)

Wednesday 20 June 1934. At Crewe station LMS 'Royal Scot' Class 6P 4-6-0 No 6119 *Lancashire Fusilier*, resplendent in Crimson Lake livery, is waiting to depart with a passenger train. A product of the North British Locomotive Co (NBL) in 1927, she would be rebuilt with a taper boiler during 1944 and be withdrawn from service by British Railways in 1963 numbered 46119. Her smoke box is carrying the shed code 15 which is the former LNWR designation for Crewe. Note the driver checking under the front buffer beam. (GB132)

Wednesday 20 June 1934. The 'Prince of Wales' Class of express passenger locomotive, introduced in 1911 to a design by Charles Bowen Cooke for the LNWR, were all constructed with superheating boilers. Construction continued until 1922 by which time two hundred and forty-six examples were in service, one last member of the class was added in 1924. Crewe Works constructed one hundred and thirty-seven examples, William Beardmore & Co of Glasgow ninety examples and the NBL twenty. One hundred of the class received names but all those from Beardmore remained nameless. Seen here at Crewe is a close up of former LNWR 'Prince of Wales' (LMS Class 4P) 4-6-0 No 25621 *Thomas Moore*. A product of Crewe Works during 1913, she would be withdrawn from service later in 1934. (GB137)

Monday 2 July 1934. Former Midland Railway Class 3 (LMS Class 3F) 0-6-0 No 3637 had been constructed as part of a batch of twenty delivered from Derby Works during 1900. Seen here at Nottingham Midland station waiting to depart with a local working, she would be withdrawn after sixty-four years of service in 1964 numbered 43637 by British Railways. Note the number 18 on her smoke box which is the former Midland Railway shed code designation for Nottingham. (GB709)

Saturday 4 August 1934. At Nottingham Midland station ex-MR (LMS Class 2P) 4-4-0 No 387 is waiting to be released from the platform. Constructed at Derby Works during 1888, she would be withdrawn from service in 1936. (GB162)

Saturday 1 September 1934. At the head of a through train at Nottingham Midland station is ex-LNWR 'Claughton' (LMS Class 5XP) 4-6-0 No 5923 *Sir Guy Calthrop*. A product of Crewe Works in 1916 and named after a former General Manager of the LNWR, she would only give nineteen years of service, being withdrawn during 1935. The four-cylinder, superheated boiler 'Claughton' class designed by Charles Bowen Cooke were introduced during 1913 specifically to handle the increasingly heavy Scottish passenger traffic over the lines with gradients such as that at Shap. A total of one hundred and thirty entered service, all from Crewe Works, with the last appearing in 1921. (GB714)

Saturday 1 September 1934. Ex-MR Class 2 (LMS Class 2F) 0-6-0 No 3383 is seen at Nottingham carriage sidings servicing area with the crew overseeing the filling of the tender with water. She is carrying the correct ex-Midland Railway shed code, 18, on her smoke box. An example of a batch of the class delivered from Sharp, Stewart & Co during 1892, she would be withdrawn in 1935. (GB180)

September 1934. In sparkling condition having exited Derby Works early in this month, Stanier three-cylinder LMS Class 4P 2-6-4 tank No 2521 is seen on the turntable at Nottingham probably during her 'running in' period. Designed specifically to work on the London, Tilbury and Southend section of the LMS, the class of thirty-seven examples spent their entire lives working on the intensive services operated out of Fenchurch Street station. This example would be withdrawn from service in 1961 numbered 42521. (GB187)

September 1934. Also seen at Nottingham carriage sidings is ex-MR Class 2 (LMS Class 2P) 4-4-0 No 353 bearing a 25, Sheffield, shed code. Constructed at Derby Works during 1883 she would give seventy years of service, being withdrawn in 1953 numbered 40353 by British Railways. (GB188)

September 1934. The crew of LMS 'Compound' Class 4P 4-4-0 No 925 seem proud to be able to pose for the photographer at Nottingham carriage sidings. In beautifully clean condition she is carrying the correct shed code plate, 18, for this shed. A product of Derby Works in 1927, she would be numbered 40925 with British Railways and be withdrawn from service during 1959. (GB189)

Friday 12 October 1934. Also in beautifully clean condition and seen at Nottingham Midland shed is ex-LNWR four-cylinder 'Claughton' (LMS Class 5P) 4-6-0 No 5932 *Sir Thomas Williams*. A product of Crewe Works during 1917, she would be withdrawn from service seven months after this photograph in April 1935 after the short working life of only eighteen years. (GB817)

Sunday 3 March 1935. The second of the William Stanier designs to enter service with the LMS in October 1933 were the Class 5 2-6-0s whose design had originated at Horwich Works. Forty examples were constructed at Crewe Works during 1933 and 1934 with No 13263, seen here at Crewe shed, being a 1933 example. Later to be numbered 2963 with the LMS and becoming 42963 with British Railways, she would be withdrawn in 1966. (GB818)

Sunday 24 March 1935. Ex-LNWR 'Claughton' No 6025 is seen here again at Derby Works prior to being withdrawn from service five months later in August 1935. (GB718)

Opposite: Sunday 28 April 1935. Ex-LNWR Charles Bowen Cooke designed 5' 6" driving wheel 4-6-2 tank No 6957, bearing a 3E Monument Lane Birmingham shed code, is waiting to depart from Rugby station. Constructed at Crewe Works in 1911 with a superheating boiler and a Belpaire firebox, she would be withdrawn during 1937. (GB721)

Above: Sunday 5 May 1935. The first examples of the William Stanier 'Jubilee' Class 5XP three-cylinder 4-6-0 locomotives entered service in May and June 1934 with increasing numbers, exiting both Crewe and Derby Works and the NBL Co in Glasgow throughout 1934, 1935 and the end of 1936 by which time one hundred and ninety-one examples had been delivered. Seen here at Derby is No 5624 which had entered service from Crewe Works seven months earlier in October 1934 and would be named *St Helena* in 1936. She is carrying a 20A Leeds shed code and is seen fitted with a vacuum pump attached to the lower slide bar and connected to the crosshead. She would later be numbered 45624 by British Railways and be withdrawn from service in 1963. (GB723)

Sunday 5 May 1935. This close up of LMS Class 4P compound 4-4-0 No 1046 shows her in ex-works condition at Derby. A product of the same works during 1924, she would be withdrawn from service in 1953. (GB820)

Monday 13 May 1935. At Nottingham shed ex-LT&SR Class 51 (LMS Class 2P) 4-4-2 tank No 2102 is carrying a 16A Nottingham shed code. Constructed by Sharp, Stewart & Co in 1900 she would be numbered 61 and named *Kentish Town* by the LT&SR, becoming No 2168 with the Midland Railway and later No 2102 with the LMS. She would be withdrawn from service in 1949. (GB213)

Saturday 8 June 1935. Seen on the turntable at Nottingham carriage sidings is ex-LNWR 'Precursor' (LMS Class 3P) 4-4-0 No 25211 *Aurania*. A product of Crewe Works during 1905, she would be withdrawn in 1936. Designed by George Whale and introduced in 1904 with a total of one hundred and thirty being constructed, the last entering service in 1907. (GB240)

Wednesday 21 August 1935. This George Whale designed ex-LNWR 'Precursor' (LMS Class 3P) 4-4-0 No 5304 *Greyhound* is seen at the carriage sidings at Nottingham. Constructed at Crewe Works during 1905, she would be withdrawn in 1947. (GB259)

Wednesday 4 September 1935. Seen near Nottingham is ex-LNWR Class G2 (LMS Class 7F) 0-8-0 No 9453 at the head of a goods train. Designed by Captain Beames and constructed during 1921 and 1922, a total of sixty examples of this powerful superheated boilered class were constructed at Crewe Works. No 9453 was a 1922 example that would become No 49453 with British Railways and be withdrawn during 1961. (GB265)

Wednesday 4 September 1935. Seen on the turntable at Nottingham carriage sidings is unnamed ex-LNWR 'Prince of Wales' (LMS Class 4P) 4-6-0 No 25834. Entering service from William Beardmore & Co in Glasgow during 1922, she would only give fourteen years of service being withdrawn in 1936. (GB268)

Friday 6 September 1935. Also seen on the turntable is ex-LNWR 'George the Fifth' (LMS Class 3P) 4-4-0 No 5339 *Henry Maudslay* which had been the product of Crewe Works during 1911 that would be withdrawn from service in 1937. (GB272)

Thursday 19 September 1935. Authorisation for the production of the William Stanier Class 5XP 'Jubilee' locomotives was given in May 1933 with the first entering service a year later in May 1934. A total of one hundred and ninety-one examples of this three-cylinder design were produced with the NBL constructing fifty members and Derby Works only contributing ten examples, the remainder coming out of Crewe Works. This close-up of an unnamed No 5608 is seen here at Nottingham shed, she would acquire the name *Gibraltar* in 1936 and be numbered 45608 with British Railways and be withdrawn during 1965. (GB275)

Sunday 13 October 1935. With the British Thomson Houston (BTH) factory in the background, LMS Class 6P 'Royal Scot' 4-6-0 No 6112 *Sherwood Forester* is at the head of a fifteen coach 'up' working as it arrives at Rugby. Constructed by the NBL in 1927, she would be rebuilt with a taper boiler during 1943 and be withdrawn from service in 1964 numbered 46112. (GB281)

Sunday 3 November 1935. At Derby Works, seen in ex-works condition and yet to enter service, is William Stanier designed Class 3P 2-6-2 tank No 142. Becoming number 40142 with British Railways, she would be withdrawn during 1961. A total of one hundred and thirty-nine were constructed between 1935 and 1938 with Derby Works delivering one hundred and fourteen examples and Crewe Works producing twenty-five members of the class. (GB691)

Sunday 3 November 1935. The ungainly looking MR Class 2000 (LMS Class 3P) 0-6-4 tanks introduced by Richard Deeley during 1907 became known as 'Flatirons' and were lacklustre performers. No 2034, seen here at Derby shed, was originally constructed during 1907 at Derby Works with a saturated steam boiler that would be replaced with a superheating boiler in 1926. She would only give thirty years of service, being withdrawn in 1937. (GB738)

Sunday 22 March 1936. At Derby shed carrying a 17A Derby shed code, ex-MR Class 1121 (LMS Class 1F) 0-6-0 tank No 1873 was the product of the same works in 1899. She would be withdrawn during 1950 numbered 41873 by British Railways. (GB291)

Monday 11 May 1936. Seen on the turntable at Nottingham carriage sidings is ex-LNWR 'Prince of Wales' (LMS Class 3P) 4-6-0 No 25671 *Arethusa* which had been the product of Crewe Works during 1916. She was destined to be withdrawn seven months after this photograph in December 1936. (GB295A)

Monday 11 May 1936. Departing from Nottingham Midland station is LMS Class 5XP 'Jubilee' 4-6-0 No 5656 *Cochrane* at the head of an 'up' working. One of only ten members of the class constructed at Derby Works in 1934, she would be withdrawn by British Railways during 1962 numbered 45656. She had been named after a Rear-Admiral who as a Captain had fought in the Napoleonic Wars. (GB307)

Tuesday 19 May 1936. At the head of a 'down' express approaching Nottingham Midland station, LMS Class 5XP 'Jubilee' 4-6-0 No 5662 _Kempenfelt_ was one of the Derby Works constructed members of the class that entered service late in 1934. Named after the British Admiral who had won the Battle of Ushant in 1781, she would be withdrawn numbered 45662 during 1962. (GB321)

Tuesday 19 May 1936. Seen accelerating away from Nottingham Midland station at the head of the 'up' 'Thames - Forth' express, LMS Class 5XP 'Jubilee' 4-6-0 No 5655 was also a Derby Works constructed member of the class, entering service in late 1934. She would acquire the name *Keith* (a British Admiral of the Fleet) in 1937 and be withdrawn numbered 45655 during 1965. (GB322)

Tuesday 9 June 1936. Being turned on the turntable at Nottingham carriage sidings is one of the early Johnson/Deeley MR Class 4 (LMS Class 4P) three-cylinder 'Compound' 4-4-0s No 1011. Constructed at Derby works during 1905 with a saturated steam boiler, she would be rebuilt in 1922 with a superheating boiler. Becoming No 41011 with British Railways, she would be withdrawn in 1951. (GB323)

Sunday 21 June 1936. At Horwich Works ex-L&YR Class 28 (LMS Class 3F) 0-6-0 No 12572 is carrying a 24F Fleetwood shed code and is awaiting attention in the works. Constructed at the same works in 1901, she would be withdrawn during 1953 numbered 52572. (GB329)

Sunday 21 June 1936. Also seen at Horwich Works, minus coupling and connecting rods, awaiting attention is ex-L&YR Class 8 (LMS Class 5P) 4-6-0 four-cylinder No 10442. Designed by George Hughes and introduced in 1908, the first batch of twenty examples were fitted with saturated steam boilers and found to be poor steamers so when further batches were constructed from 1921 they were fitted with superheating boilers and Walschaerts valve gear, these changes improved their performance. No 10442 had entered service in 1923 and would become the penultimate member of the class to be withdrawn from service in 1950. (GB330)

Wednesday 8 July 1936. Seen departing from Carlisle station with the 'down' Glasgow portion of the 'Midday Scot' is LMS Class 7P 'Princess Royal' 4-6-2 No 6207 *Princess Arthur of Connaught* bearing a 1B Camden shed code. The product of Crewe Works during 1935, she would be withdrawn in 1961 numbered 46207. The first of the William Stanier designs to come to fruition with the premier member of the class No 6200 *The Princess Royal* entering service during July 1933 being followed by twelve further members of the class between 1933 and 1935. (GB340)

Wednesday 8 July 1936. The locomotive seen arriving at Carlisle, No 20087, is possibly working a train from the Cockermouth and Keswick line as she was based at Penrith shed at this time. Constructed by Neilson & Co during 1871 as part of a delivery for the Midland Railway of its 2-4-0 Class 890, she would be rebuilt on several occasions finally being withdrawn early the following year, 1937. (GB342)

Saturday 22 August 1936. With the 'up' 'Thames - Forth' working in tow, ex-MR Class 2 (LMS Class 2P) 4-4-0 No 551 is seen piloting LMS Class 4P 'Compound' 4-4-0 No 1051 as it departs from Nottingham Midland station. No 551 had been the product of Derby Works during 1919 that would be withdrawn in 1953 numbered 40551. No 1051 was also the product of Derby Works from 1924 that would only give thirty years of service, being withdrawn in 1954. (GB386)

Tuesday 15 September 1936. Seen on the turntable at Nottingham carriage sidings is ex-MR Class 2 (LMS Class 2P) 4-4-0 No 477 which had been constructed by Beyer, Peacock & Co during 1919 and would give only thirty-two years of service being withdrawn in 1951. (GB400)

Sunday 8 November 1936. Seen at Derby are the graceful lines of double-framed ex-MR Class 700 (LMS Class 1F) 0-6-0 No 22822. Designed by Matthew Kirtley and introduced during 1869, over three hundred examples were constructed by a number of manufacturers. No 22822 was the product of the Vulcan Foundry during 1873 that would be rebuilt during 1922 with a Belpaire firebox and withdrawn after seventy-four years of service in 1947. (GB416)

Monday 25 January 1937. Seen climbing away from Nottingham London Road Junction with an 'up' passenger train, whose first vehicle is a twelve-wheeled carriage, is LMS Class 4P 'Compound' 4-4-0 No 1060. Constructed at Derby Works during 1924, she would be renumbered 41060 with British Railways and be withdrawn in 1958. (GB417)

Monday 26 April 1937. LMS Class 3P 4-4-2 tank No 2121 is accelerating away from Nottingham London Road Junction on the line to Melton Mowbray with a four coach 'up' 'local'. Constructed by Nasmyth, Wilson & Co during 1925 to work the intensive LT&SR services, she was dispersed when the Stanier three-cylinder Class 4P 2-6-4 tanks were introduced for these services. She would be later numbered 1939 with the LMS becoming No 41939 with British Railways and be withdrawn in 1959. (GB428)

Tuesday 25 May 1937. The driver of ex-LNWR 'Precursor' (LMS Class 3P) 4-4-0 No 25292 *Medusa* is attending to the operation of the vacuum controlled turntable at Nottingham carriage sidings. Entering service from Crewe Works during 1905, *Medusa* would be withdrawn in 1945. (GB457)

Saturday 5 June 1937. At Nottingham carriage sidings, ex-LNWR 'George Fifth' (LMS Class 3P) 4-4-0 No 25389 *Eclipse* is waiting for her next duty. Constructed at Crewe Works during 1913, she would be withdrawn from service later in this month, June 1937. (GB455)

Saturday 5 June 1937. Ex-LNWR 'Cauliflower' (LMS Class 2F) 0-6-0 No 8492 is being positioned on the turntable at Nottingham carriage sidings in preparation for turning, she would become number 58389 with British Railways and be withdrawn in 1953. Designed by Francis Webb and introduced during 1880 as their '18" Goods Class', a total of three hundred and ten examples were constructed, all at Crewe Works, the last appearing in 1902. (GB464)

Saturday 31 July 1937. The design of this double-framed locomotive seen at Nottingham London Road Low Level station is the work of Matthew Kirtley for the Midland Railway. Ex-MR Class 700 (LMS Class 2F) 0-6-0 No 22846 had been constructed by Dübs & Co in 1873. The class extended to over three hundred members constructed not only by Dübs but by Kitson & Co, Neilson, Reid & Co, the Vulcan Foundry, John Fowler Ltd and also the Midland's own Derby Works. She would become No 58111 with British Railways and would finally be withdrawn after seventy-six years of service in 1949. (GB506)

Saturday 31 July 1937. At Nottingham London Road Low Level station, ex-MR Class 2 (LMS Class 2F) 0-6-0 No 3551 sees her fireman trimming the coal in the tender prior to departure at the head of a local 'stopper'. Constructed during 1897 as part of a batch of twenty-five ordered from Sharp, Stewart & Co, she would be rebuilt in 1945 with a Belpaire firebox and be withdrawn after sixty years' service during 1957, numbered 58288 by British Railways. (GB759)

Saturday 31 July 1937. The locomotive seen here undertaking pilot duties at Nottingham London Road Low Level station is already seventy-one years old, having been constructed at Derby Works during 1866. Designed by Matthew Kirtley as Class 156 for the Midland Railway to haul express passenger traffic, No 20002 was originally numbered 158A by them and spent the last years of her life on station pilot duties. She is seen here carrying a 16A Nottingham shed code. Withdrawn during 1947, she was restored for display purposes and finally became part of the National Collection and can now be seen on display at the Midland Railway Centre at Butterley. (GB760)

Sunday 10 October 1937. In ex-works condition and seen standing at Crewe Works is ex-LNWR 'Coal Tank' (LMS Class 2F) No 7823 which had been constructed at the same works during 1892. She would give fifty-five years of service, being withdrawn in 1947. (GB513)

Sunday 10 October 1937. At Crewe shed LMS Class 7P 'Princess Coronation' 4-6-2 No 6221 *Queen Elizabeth* is only four months into her operational life of twenty-six years hauling express passenger traffic on the West Coast Main Line between London and Scotland. The second member of the class, she entered service in June of this year from Crewe Works in the streamlined form seen here, this would be removed during 1946 and she would be withdrawn from service in 1963. (GB764)

Sunday 10 October 1937. Standing outside Crewe Works is ex-LNWR 'Cauliflower' (LMS Class 2F) 0-6-0 No 8602 which is nearing the end of her working life as she would be withdrawn two months after this photograph in December 1937. She had been constructed at the same works in 1901. (GB766)

Sunday 13 February 1938. Seen in brand new ex-works condition at Crewe Works, LMS Class 3P 2-6-2 tank No 202 is yet to be put into service. Becoming No 40202 with British Railways, she would be withdrawn in 1962. (GB518)

Sunday 13 February 1938. At Crewe Works LMS Class 7P 'Princess Royal' 4-6-2 No 6209 *Princess Beatrice* is seen equipped with an indicator shelter prior to trials being carried out. Constructed at the same works in 1935, she would become No 46209 with British Railways and be withdrawn during 1962. (GB520)

Sunday 13 February 1938. LMS Class 6P 'Royal Scot' 4-6-0 No 6170 *British Legion* is seen in the yard at Crewe shed. Beginning life as an order from the LMS to the North British Locomotive Co and the Superheater Co to construct a locomotive powered by a high pressure water-tube boiler, this was erected on a 'Royal Scot' frame and running gear and emerged from the NBL in December 1929 numbered 6399 and named *Fury*. During her trials in February 1930 a boiler tube burst killing an observer on the footplate and after repairs and further trials were carried out it was deemed to be an unsuccessful experiment. The locomotive was rebuilt during 1935 with a conventional boiler and entered service in October of that year. She would be withdrawn from service during 1962. (GB767)

Below: Monday 2 May 1938. Ex-LNWR 'Precursor' (LMS Class 3P) 4-4-0 No 25319 *Bucephalus* is seen here on the turntable at Nottingham carriage sidings. A product of Crewe Works during 1906, she would be one of the last of the class to be withdrawn from service in 1940. (GB532)

Opposite: Sunday 31 July 1938. With the British Thomson Houston factory in the background, LMS Class 5P5F 4-6-0 No 5121 is seen arriving at Rugby with an express consisting of a very mixed rake of coaches. Constructed at the Vulcan Foundry in 1935 she would be withdrawn during 1964 numbered 45121. (GB546)

Monday 15 August 1938. With a long train of loaded mineral wagons, ex-LNWR Class G2 (LMS Class 7F) 0-8-0 No 9408 is working hard near Hillmorton Junction with an 'up' on the Northampton line. Constructed at Crewe Works during 1921, she would be withdrawn numbered 49408 by British Railways in 1962. (GB543)

Sunday 25 September 1938. Webb designed 18" 0-6-2 tank No 6926 is seen in ex-works condition at Crewe Works, a product of the same works during 1902 she would be withdrawn in 1948. A total of eighty examples were all constructed at Crewe Works between 1898 and 1902. (GB577B)

Above and Opposite: Sunday 25 September 1938. The photographer has taken the opportunity to capture these two shots of LMS Class 5XP 'Patriot' 4-6-0 No 5541 *Duke of Sutherland* at Crewe station whilst it was waiting to take over a train. A product of Crewe Works during 1933, she would acquire the name from 'Claughton' Class locomotive No 5903 that had been withdrawn from service earlier in 1933. As British Railways No 45541 she would be withdrawn from service in 1962. (GB573/776)

Sunday 25 September 1938. Bearing an 18B Westhouses shed code, LMS Class 8F 2-8-0 No 8094 is seen at Crewe. Constructed at the Vulcan Foundry in 1937 and requisitioned by the War Department during 1941, she would be numbered WD606 and later WD70606 by them and sent to work in Persia. Returned to British Railways during 1949 and numbered 48094, she would be withdrawn from service in 1965. (GB661)

Sunday 9 October 1938. LMS Class 4F 0-6-0 No 4236 had been constructed at Derby Works during 1926 and would be withdrawn in 1964 numbered 44236. Seen here at Derby shed she is carrying a 15A Wellingborough shed code. (GB678)

Sunday 9 October 1938. Also seen at Derby Works is brand new, not yet in service, LMS Class 4MT 2-6-4 tank No 2636. Numbered 42636 she would be withdrawn from service twenty-five years later in 1963. This William Stanier design was an improved version of the earlier Fowler tanks with over two hundred examples being constructed. (GB682)

Sunday 26 February 1939. At Crewe ex-LNWR Class G2A (LMS Class 7F) 0-8-0 No 9237 had just re-entered service after being rebuilt from Class G1 during the previous month. Originally constructed at the same works in 1914, she would give a total of thirty-five years of service, being withdrawn during 1949. (GB591)

Monday 24 April 1939. Seen at speed north of Rugby near Brinklow at the head of the 'up' 'Merseyside Express' is LMS Class 7P 'Princess Royal' 4-6-2 No 6208 *Princess Helena Victoria.* A product of Crewe Works during 1935, she would be withdrawn in 1962 numbered 46208. (GB780)

Tuesday 7 May 1939. At Stafford shed, resident ex-LNWR 'Prince of Wales' (LMS Class 4P) 4-6-0 No 25775 had been constructed during 1921 by William Beardmore & Co and was one of the unnamed members of the class. She would be withdrawn in 1947. (GB601)

Tuesday 7 May 1939. Seen shunting wagons at Crewe Works is ex-LNWR 0-4-2 Crane Tank No 3248. Constructed at the same works during 1893, she would be withdrawn in 1947. Originally constructed as part of a class of 0-4-0 saddle tanks designed by John Ramsbottom, a total of eight members of the class would be constructed as 0-4-2 Crane Tanks. (GB602)

Tuesday 7 May 1939. This close-up taken at Crewe shed shows unrebuilt LMS Class 6P 'Royal Scot' 4-6-0 No 6139 *The Welch Regiment* as she awaits her next duty. A product of the NBL during 1927 and originally named *Ajax*, she would be renamed in 1936. Rebuilt during 1944 with a taper boiler, she would be withdrawn from service in 1962 numbered 46139. (GB781)

Above: Tuesday 7 May 1939. Beyer, Peacock & Co constructed 'Garratt' 2-6-0+0-6-2 No 7973 is seen at Crewe. Weighing in at a massive 152.5 tons and constructed in Manchester in 1930, a total of thirty-three examples entered service with the LMS, three during 1927 and the remainder in 1930. No 7973 would be withdrawn from service in 1957. (GB782)

Opposite: Tuesday 28 May 1939. Seen bursting from the south portal of Kilsby tunnel on the West Coast Main Line is LMS Class 6P 'Royal Scot' 4-6-0 No 6141 *The North Staffordshire Regiment.* Constructed by the NBL during 1927, she would be rebuilt with a taper boiler in 1950 and be withdrawn in 1964. She had originally carried the name *Caledonian* which she lost in 1936 when renaming took place. (GB785)

Sunday 6 August 1939. With at least twelve coaches behind her tender, LMS Class 6P 'Royal Scot' 4-6-0 No 6124 *London Scottish* **makes a fine sight near Rugby with a special working. Another example of the NBL-built members of the class from 1927, she would be rebuilt with a taper boiler in 1943 and be withdrawn from service during 1962 numbered 46124. (GB610)**

Sunday 6 August 1939. Also seen near Rugby is LMS Class 7P 'Princess Coronation' 4-6-2 No 6230 *Duchess of Buccleuch* getting into her stride with another train of at least twelve coaches. Constructed at Crewe Works in 1938, she would be withdrawn after twenty-five years of service during 1963 numbered 46230. (GB614)

Sunday 20 August 1939. Seen at Crewe Works is ex-LNWR Webb designed 2-4-2 tank No 6603 which was a product of the same works in 1891 that would become number 46603 with British Railways and be withdrawn during 1951. (GB612)

Sunday 20 August 1939. In sparkling ex-works condition at Crewe Works is ex-LNWR 0-4-2 Crane Tank No 3249. A product of the same works in 1894, she would be withdrawn from service during 1947. (GB788)

Want more...?

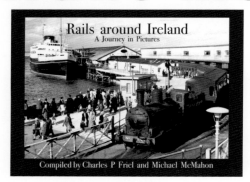

Rails around Ireland

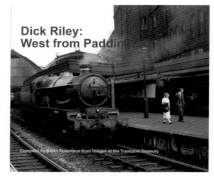

Dick Riley: West from Paddington

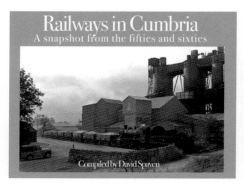

Railways in Cumbria

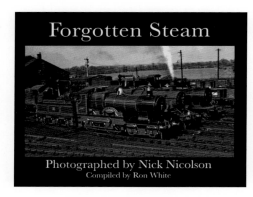

Forgotten Steam

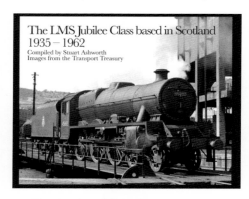

The LMS Jubilee Class based in Scotland 1935 - 1962

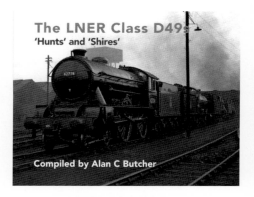

The LNER Class D49s - 'Hunts' and 'Shires'